CELEBRATING

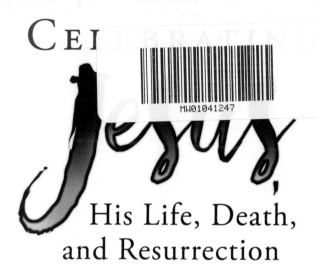

Jesus,

His Life, Death, and Resurrection

MEDITATIONS FOR
LENT AND EASTER

Celebrating Jesus, His Life, Death, and Resurrection
Meditations for Lent and Easter

Scripture quotations used in this book were taken from the following:

D3899

ISBN: 978-1-68434-028-6

© 2018 Warner Press, Inc.

All rights reserved

Made in USA

INTRODUCTION

*F*or those of you who may not be familiar with its meaning, Lent lasts from Ash Wednesday to Holy Saturday. Sundays are not counted as part of the 40 days—40 being significant throughout the Bible. Moses spent 40 days on Mount Sinai; Elijah spent 40 days and nights walkng to Mount Horeb; God sent 40 days and nights of rain in the great flood; the Israelites wandered 40 years in the desert, traveling to the Promised Land; Jonah's prophecy of judgment on Nineveh gave them 40 days to repent; Jesus spent 40 days in the wilderness, being tempted by Satan.

Lent, traditionally, is a time for believers to focus intentionally on the great sacrifice Christ made—through prayer, Bible study, repentance, fasting, and self-denial. For many, the goal of Lent is to develop a closer relationship with God and to strengthen their faith.

IV

Day 1

Ash Wednesday

*O*ur God is ever present in
the blossoming of spring,

For this season bears a promise
that makes the soul sing.

A promise that transcends
the shadows of earth's night

And assures that we will live
again where all is peace and light.

—CHRIS AHLEMANN

*If anyone is in Christ, the new creation has
come: The old has gone, the new is here!*

2 CORINTHIANS 5:17 (NIV)

Day 2

With His hand He gently leads us to greener pastures.

With His heart He watches over us and sets a banquet table before us.

With His life He gave His all... till our cup overflows.

—Linda E. Knight

The Lord is my shepherd; I shall not want.

Psalm 23:1

Day 3

*G*od loves me, but doesn't pencil in conditions that I have to fulfill to earn that love.

He protects me, but allows me to operate with free will so that I can choose Him above all else.

To prove His love, God gave me the most precious gift imaginable: the life of His beloved Son.

And **that** my friend is enough.

—CAROL MEAD

God commendeth his love toward us,
in that, while we were yet sinners,
Christ died for us.

ROMANS 5:8

Day 4

Deep inside me I hesitate, I think, because it seems incredible that God wants so much for me to be with Him.

On a dark and excruciatingly painful Friday a Father sacrificed His Son for me.

Knowing how weak, and vain, and material and fearful I am, He still chose to sacrifice His Son.

And because He did, I'm no longer an orphan, but a child of the great, and good, and powerful God.

—Carol Mead

I will not leave you as orphans; I will come to you.... On that day you will realize that I am in my Father, and you are in me, and I am in you. Whoever has my commands and obeys them, he is the one who loves me.

John 14:18-21 (NIV)

Day 5

Sunday

Marvelous grace of our loving Lord, Grace that exceeds our sin and our guilt! Yonder on Calvary's mount outpoured—There where the blood of the Lamb was spilt.

Grace, grace, God's grace, Grace that will pardon and cleanse within; Grace, grace, God's grace, Grace that is greater than all our sin!

—Julia H. Johnston

(Grace Greater than Our Sin)

By grace are ye saved through faith; and that not of yourselves: it is the gift of God.

Ephesians 2:8

Extend grace (undeserved favor) to someone this week. Give a gift of your time, your talents, your love, to someone who needs encouragement.

Day 6

He wrestled with justice that we might have rest; He wept and mourned that we might laugh and rejoice; He was betrayed that we might go free; was apprehended that we might escape; He was condemned that we might be justified, and was killed that we might live. He wore a crown of thorns that we might wear a crown of glory; and was nailed to the cross with His arms wide open to show…how completely He will receive us into His bosom.

—JOHN BUNYAN (PARAPHRASED)

He was wounded for our transgressions, he was bruised for our iniquities: the chastisement of our peace was upon him; and with his stripes we are healed.

ISAIAH 53:5

Pray for persons in need of healing— spiritual, physical, emotional.

Day 7

If a mountain can bear witness of God's majesty and a flock of birds can wing His praises across the sky; if a flower can lift its petals to God and a galaxy of stars can sing of His glory, then…so can I!

—Linda E. Knight

I will be exalted in the earth.

Psalm 46:10

Day 8

The death of Jesus was not the death
of a martyr, it was the revelation
of the eternal heart of God.

—Oswald Chambers

For God so loved the world, that he gave
his only begotten Son, that whosoever
believeth in him should not perish, but
have everlasting life. For God sent not his
Son into the world to condemn the world;
but that the world through him might be
saved.

John 3:16-17

Day 9

A life well lived
makes yesterday
a treasure
and fills tomorrow
with promise.

—LINDA E. KNIGHT

*Seek ye first the kingdom of God, and his
righteousness; and all these things shall be
added unto you.*

MATTHEW 6:33

Day 10

In His life, Christ is an example,
showing us how to live;

In His death, He is a sacrifice,
satisfying for our sins;

In His resurrection, a conqueror;
In His ascension, a king;
In His intercession, a high priest.

—MARTIN LUTHER

The Son of man came not to be ministered unto, but to minister, and to give his life a ransom for many.

MATTHEW 20:28

Day 11

On His journey…
  His gaze was steady,
  His words moved multitudes,
  His miracles healed many.

In the garden…
  His heart was heavy,
  His prayers were fervent,
  His tears ran deep.

On the cross…
  His life was sacrificed,
  His body broken,
  His work was done.

Still…
It's there at the cross,
amidst such great suffering,
that Jesus looked out and loved us all.

All that for me.
All that for you.
All that for **Love**.

—Linda E. Knight

Day 12

Sunday

So I'll cherish the old rugged cross,
'Til my trophies at last I lay doen'
I willl cling to the old rugged cross,
And exchange it some day for a
crown.

And being found in fashion as a man, he humbled himself, and became obedient unto death, even the death of the cross.

PHILIPPIANS 2:8

Pray for at least one friend to whom the cross has no significance. Ask God to help you share Jesus with that person soon.

Day 13

Never again would the cross
haughtily boast of death's cruel power.

Although blameless and pure,
Jesus Christ had offered His life
for man's release from sin,
and had willingly died on the cross.

But death, in all its might,
could not hold Him down.

Christ arose the victor to take
His place beside the Father.

And the message of His empty cross
began to spread throughout the world:

Because I live, ye shall live also.

JOHN 14:19

Day 14

Jesus Christ came to do what no human being can do: He came to redeem men, to alter their disposition, to plant in them the Holy Spirit, to make them new creatures.

His teaching has no meaning for us unless we enter into His life by means of His death. The cross is the great central point.

—Oswald Chambers

For God sent Jesus to take the punishment for our sins and to satisfy God's anger against us. We are made right with God when we believe that Jesus shed his blood, sacrificing his life for us.

Romans 3:25 (NLT)

Day 15

To a world seeking faith, hope,
and love, Easter's glorious tidings
are God's timeless answer.

He died for all, that they which live
should not...live unto themselves,
but unto him which died for them,
and rose again.

2 CORINTHIANS 5:15

15

Day 16

We sometimes take for granted the wonderful, foundational peace that we enjoy as Christians because Jesus rose
from the dead.

We need not worry about that unpredictable day of our death, for Christ has made that trip already and arranged for our safe passage.

The joy of our Easter celebration comes from a God who has provided everything for us—spiritually and physically.

Is it any wonder that we rejoice?

—Jennie Bishop

My God shall supply all your need.

Philippians 4:19

Day 17

In this day and age it is easy to take for granted the everyday presence of Jesus in our hearts.

How fortunate we are to have Him with us all the time—but how often we forget to walk away from mundane distractions long enough to throw down our garments of praise and honor, our branches of love and esteem, welcoming Him with shouts of "Hosanna!"

—Jennie Bishop

Hosanna! Blessed is he who comes in the name of the Lord!

Mark 11:9 (NIV)

Day 18

I look at the cross, and wonder how anyone can love so much. It's a mystery, but I think I can live with it. Forever.

—Carol Mead

For Christ also hath once suffered for sins, ...that he might bring us to God.

1 Peter 3:18

Day 19

Sunday

Redeemer, Savior, friend of man
 Once ruined by the fall,

Thou hast devised salvation's plan,
 For Thou hast died for all.

Blessed be the name! Blessed
 be the name!
Blessed be the name of the Lord!

—W.H. Clark

(Blessed Be the Name)

*Blessed be your glorious name, and may it be
exalted above all blessing and praise.*

Nehemiah 9:5

**Praise God for the everlasting light
He brought to our hearts.**

Day 20

*O*nly Christ could ransom us, only He was worthy to repay the debt He never owed—alone on the altar—Calvary's Lamb.

—RANDY VADER

For there is one God and one mediator between God and mankind, the man Christ Jesus, who gave himself as a ransom for all people.

1 TIMOTHY 2:5–6

Day 21

What's Easter,
  but God's promise—

His ever-loving way
of showing us that sunny skies
forever follow gray,

that sorrow leads to victory,
hope conquers all despair,
and that it is His perfect plan
to keep us in His care!

The Lord has turned all our
sunsets into sunrise.

—Gregory the Great

When He came, there was no light.
When He left, there was no darkness.

Day 22

When I see a roadblock that causes me stress,
God created an opening, a way to bless.

When I find it difficult to take a stand,
God promises to hold my hand.

When it seems the world's gone mad and grim,
God beckons me to make more room for Him.

When I'm in doubt and clouds block my view,
God shines a ray of hope making all things new.

When life moves so quickly I can barely keep
pace, God provides an extra measure of grace.

When I see only responsibility and duty,
God displays a sunset to remind me of beauty.

When summertime ends and the flowers all die,
help me, dear God, to see life through Your eyes.
Amen.

—KAY CAMPBELL

Day 23

*O*nly a nail-scarred hand could pay the debt that sets us free. We are redeemed!

O LORD, thou hast pleaded the causes of my soul; thou hast redeemed my life.

LAMENTATIONS 3:58

Jesus knew it was not a king we needed...
but a Savior,
not an earthly ruler...
but an eternal Lord.

For God so loved the world, that he gave his only begotten Son, that whosoever believeth in him should not perish, but have everlasting life.

JOHN 3:16

Day 24

Just as I am, without one plea
But that Thy blood was shed for me,
And that Thou bid'st me come to Thee,
O Lamb of God, I come!

—Charlotte Elliott

(Just As I Am)

He has rescued us from the dominion of darkness and brought us into the kingdom of the Son he loves, in whom we have redemption, the forgiveness of sins.

Colossians 1:13-14 (NIV)

Day 25

Although blameless and pure,
Jesus Christ offered His life
for man's release from sin
and willingly died on the cross.

Christ rose the victor
to take His place beside the Father.

The message of His empty cross?

Because I live, ye shall live also.

JOHN 14:19

Day 26

Sunday

Tell of the cross where they nailed Him,
   writhing in anguish and pain;

Tell of the grave where they laid Him,
   tell how He liveth again…

Lord, may I always remember
Love paid the ransom for me.

—FANNY J. CROSBY

(TELL ME THE STORIES OF JESUS)

*There is one God, and one mediator
between God and men, the man Christ
Jesus; who gave himself a ransom for all.*

1 TIMOTHY 2:5-6

**Ask God to help you "tell His story"
to someone today. Praise Him for
His love that set you free.**

Day 27

The story was not over when Christ died.... It was only the prelude to the glorious event of Easter when mankind received its greatest treasure—the proof of life eternal.

Being made perfect, he became the author of eternal salvation unto all them that obey him.

Hebrews 5:9

Day 28

Now He lives as the Lily of the Valley, the Rose of Sharon, the Fairest of Ten Thousand.

As we remember His death and resurrection this Easter, may we all open our hearts to the new life, the flowering faith that He begins and will be faithful to complete in our lives!

—Jennie Bishop

But the Lord is faithful, and he will strengthen and protect you.

2 Thessalonians 3:3 (NIV)

Day 29

Unless a kernel of wheat falls to the ground and dies, it remains only a single seed.

JOHN 12:24 (NIV)

How eloquently our Lord mirrored His death and resurrection in this statement.

Like a seed He fell to the ground, He was buried; He died.

But that was not the end.

Like a new flower He rose up again, causing faith to blossom and eternal life to be rooted and secured forever, for all of us.

Day 30

Before His crucifixion,
Jesus prepared the disciples
for His departure.

He promised He would not
leave them comfortless.

He would send the Spirit
to remind them of all
He had taught them.

Then, if they would keep
His commandments
and love Him,
they would be filled with the Spirit.

Even the Spirit of truth…
for he dwelleth with you, and shall be in you
(JOHN 14:17)…. And in us!

Day 31

*E*aster plants a new song of
praise in our hearts of God's
unending love and peace, of
ever-growing joy and promise.

—ANNE CALODICH FONE

I will praise you, Lord my God,
with all my heart; I will glorify
your name forever.

PSALM 86:12 (NIV)

Day 32

Jesus, keep me near the cross—
There a precious fountain,
Free to all, a healing stream,
Flows from Calvary's mountain.

Near the cross! O Lamb of God,
Bring its scenes before me;
Help me walk from day to day
With its shadow o'er me.

Day 33

Sunday

Near the cross I'll watch and wait,
  Hoping, trusting ever,
  'Til I reach the golden strand
  Just beyond the river.

  In the cross, in the cross,
  Be my glory ever,
  'Til my raptured soul shall find
  Rest beyond the river.

—FANNY J. CROSBY

(NEAR THE CROSS)

*May I never boast except in the cross of our
Lord Jesus Christ, through which the world has
been crucified to me, and I to the world.*

GALATIANS 6:14 (NIV)

**Thank God for His faithfulness, His
strength, His protection**

Day 34

If we are going to live to the fullest as children of God, we must be in the business of sacrificing. A sacrifice is not something we have plenty of or something we don't want. It is the opposite. It may be something costly and of great value; something we may not have plenty of. That's what makes it a sacrifice and challenging to let go of. We each have a temple that houses our spirit and God wants it clean; He wants our bodies!

It is within reason that we offer our bodies as "living" sacrifices. Trust that when God sets a fire on your sacrifice it is to burn away the dross and refine you, not to destroy you. You will rise from your sacrificial offering as pure gold, tried, and proven.

—JUDY LITTLEJOHN

Do you not know that your bodies are temples of the Holy Spirit? …You are not your own.

(1 CORINTHIANS 6:19, NIV)

Day 35

*J*esus renews our spirits.
He wipes our slates clean.
He sees right through us.
He searches our motives.
He lifts us up, He sets us free.
He creates within us a clean heart…
And we will live with Him, eternally.

—LINDA E. KNIGHT

*I press on toward the goal to win the prize
for which God has called me heavenward in
Christ Jesus*

PHILIPPIANS 3:14 (NIV).

Day 36

Morning comes again.
Nothing can hold it back!
Tragedy may prolong
the night of anguish,
but dawn will come again.

The crucifixion dropped a mantle
of gloom over Jesus' disciples,
and they wondered if the night
of despair would ever end.

Then morning came
and Jesus, the risen Lord,
was there to lift the veil of darkness.
Death's night could not hold Him!

He is risen, as he said.

MATTHEW 28:6

Day 37

Maundy Thursday

Ponder for a moment
the meaning of the Lord's Supper—
our Lord's sacrifice reflected
in the breaking of the bread
and sharing of the cup.

In that moment we are reminded
that Christ's coming to us a Savior
was by way of the cross.

This Easter, may Christ's gracious
presence melt our indifference and
draw us into a oneness with Him
as we experience afresh the tragedy
of Calvary.

This do in remembrance of me.

1 CORINTHIANS 11:24

Day 38

Good Friday

With lines of love
and promise,

With etchings
of grace and mercy,
in blood and sweat and tears...

He has etched us all
on the palm of His hand.

—LINDA E. KNIGHT

*And Jesus, moved with compassion, put
forth his hand and touched him.*

MARK 1:41

Day 39

It is finished! What three words could better express the work of Christ's death and resurrection?

There is no more to be said—nothing we can add to Christ's sacrifice to gain God's favor.

Our imperfection was proved by our inability to keep God's magnificent law; thus the mighty Gospel has come to make us worthy of being called children of God!

Let us live our lives as though we believe that this work is finished, acting in obedience with joy because of our love for the Lord.

—LINDA E. KNIGHT

It is finished!

JOHN 19:30 (NIV)

Day 40

Easter Sunday

He lives, He lives, Christ Jesus lives today!
He walks with me and talks with me along life's narrow way.
He lives, He lives, salvation to impart!
You ask me how I know He lives?
He lives within my heart.

—Alfred H. Ackley

I am the Living One; I was dead, and now look, I am alive for ever and ever!

Revelation 1:18 (niv)

Day 41

The Monday after Easter

Oh give thanks to the LORD, for he is good;

for his steadfast love endures forever!

*Let Israel say, "His steadfast love endures
forever."*

The LORD is my strength and my song;

he has become my salvation.

Glad songs of salvation

are in the tents of the righteous:

"The right hand of the LORD does valiantly,

the right hand of the LORD exalts,

the right hand of the LORD does valiantly!"

I shall not die, but I shall live,

and recount the deeds of the LORD.

The LORD has disciplined me severely,

but he has not given me over to death.

PSALM 118:1-2. 14-18 (ESV)

Day 42

The Tuesday after Easter

Then shall come to pass the saying that is written:

"Death is swallowed up in victory."

"O death, where is your victory?
O death, where is your sting?"

The sting of death is sin, and the power of sin is the law. But thanks be to God, who gives us the victory through our Lord Jesus Christ. Therefore, my beloved brothers, be steadfast, immovable, always abounding in the work of the Lord, knowing that in the Lord your labor is not in vain.

1 CORINTHIANS 15:54-58 (ESV)

Day 43

The Wednesday after Easter

Open to me the gates of righteousness,
    that I may enter through them
    and give thanks to the LORD.
This is the gate of the LORD;
    the righteous shall enter through it.
I thank you that you have answered me
    and have become my salvation.
The stone that the builders rejected
    has become the cornerstone.
This is the LORD's doing;
    it is marvelous in our eyes.
This is the day that the LORD has made;
    let us rejoice and be glad in it.

PSALM 118:19–24 (ESV)

Day 44

The Thursday after Easter

And they devoted themselves to the apostles' teaching and the fellowship, to the breaking of bread and the prayers. And awe came upon every soul, and many wonders and signs were being done through the apostles. And all who believed were together and had all things in common. And they were selling their possessions and belongings and distributing the proceeds to all, as any had need. And day by day, attending the temple together and breaking bread in their homes, they received their food with glad and generous hearts, praising God and having favor with all the people. And the Lord added to their number day by day those who were being saved.

ACTS 2:42–47 (ESV)